STAGE 2

Elephant Families

ARTHUR DORROS

HarperCollinsPublishers

For more information about elephants and to find out how to help protect them, contact:

IUCN, World Conservation Union
Avenue Mont Blanc
1196 Gland
Switzerland

Conservation International
Suite 1000
1015 18th Street NW
Washington, DC 20036

Wildlife Conservation International
195th Street and Southern Boulevard
Bronx, NY 10460

National Geographic Society
17th and M Streets NW
Washington, DC 20036

African Wildlife Foundation
1717 Massachusetts Avenue NW
Washington, DC 20036

World Wildlife Fund
1250 24th Street NW
Washington, DC 20037

There are also organizations in almost all African countries.

The *Let's-Read-and-Find-Out Science* series was originated by Dr. Franklyn M. Branley, Astronomer Emeritus and former Chairman of the American Museum—Hayden Planetarium, and was formerly co-edited by him and Dr. Roma Gans, Professor Emeritus of Childhood Education, Teachers College, Columbia University. Text and illustrations for each of the books in the series are checked for accuracy by an expert in the relevant field. For a complete catalog of Let's-Read-and-Find-Out Science books, write to HarperCollins Children's Books, 10 East 53rd Street, New York, NY 10022.

Let's Read-and-Find-Out Science is a registered trademark of HarperCollins Publishers.

Elephant Families
Copyright © 1994 by Arthur Dorros

Typography by Christine Kettner
1 2 3 4 5 6 7 8 9 10 ❖
First Edition

Library of Congress Cataloging-in-Publication Data
Dorros, Arthur.
    Elephant families / Arthur Dorros.
       p.   cm. — (Let's-read-and-find-out science. Stage 2)
    Summary: Describes the unique qualities, status as an endangered species, and familial behavior of elephants.
    ISBN 0-06-022948-9. — ISBN 0-06-022949-7 (lib. bdg.)
    ISBN 0-06-445122-4 (pbk.)
    1. Elephants—Juvenile literature.   2. Elephants—Behavior—Juvenile literature.   3. Familial behavior in animals—Juvenile literature.
[1. Elephants.] I. Title. II. Series.
QL737.P98D66 1994
599.6'1—dc20

92-30972
CIP
AC

For Alex

With special thanks to Sandy Andelman

Out on the grasslands of Africa, a baby elephant is born. Mother helps the baby stand up. Sisters, brothers, cousins, aunts, and grandmother watch. They are all part of a family. Elephants live in families.

The baby takes its first wobbly steps. Big sister helps the baby along with her trunk. She helps take care of the baby. She is a baby-sitter.

Sometimes the baby-sitter is a cousin or an aunt. Almost all baby elephants have baby-sitters.

You can tell elephants apart by differences in the shapes and sizes of ears and tusks. Tusks grow larger as elephants grow older.

The baby drinks milk from its mother. The older elephants eat grass, seeds, fruit, leaves, even branches and tree bark.

Elephants eat almost all day. An elephant can eat more than three hundred pounds of food each day. You would need to eat a lot, too, if you weighed three or four tons like a grown elephant. That's as much as a large truck!

Elephants often wander far to find enough to eat. An elephant family may walk forty miles a day, looking for food.

Grandmother elephant leads the way. She knows where to find the best food. The other elephants follow her. Each elephant family is led by the oldest female elephant.

Elephants can walk very quietly.
The bottoms of their feet are soft,
and elephants walk carefully on their
toes! A family of elephants could walk
right by you and you wouldn't hear
them.

Elephants are surefooted. They can
walk on logs or narrow trails.

Mother and big sister help the
baby up a steep bank. They show the
baby where the trail is.

Grandmother leads the family to trees full of fruit. She remembers how to get here for ripe fruit every year.

The elephants shake the trees with their trunks and tusks. A trunk is like a nose and hand combined. Elephants can pick leaves or peel fruit with their trunks faster than we could with our hands. Tusks are useful too. Elephants use them to dig, to push over branches or trees, and to strip off bark to eat.

The small elephants wait for fruit to drop from the trees. Babies run and play. A baby-sitter pushes apart two babies who are banging heads too hard, playing.

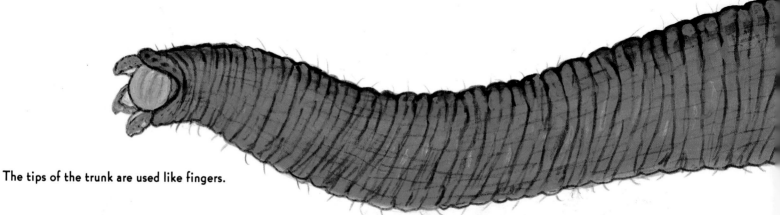

The tips of the trunk are used like fingers.

Suddenly the elephants spread their ears and hold their trunks in the air, sniffing. They stand perfectly still.

They hear and smell lions. Lions could attack a baby elephant. The babies stand in the middle of the circle of big sisters, brothers, mothers, aunts, and cousins.

Grandmother elephant raises her trunk and trumpets loudly. The lions disappear into the shadows. Not many animals will bother the big elephants.

Some elephants live in wet forests. But this family lives in dry country. They travel far to find water.

The bigger elephants dig holes in a riverbed. A little bit of water seeps into the holes from the wet sand below.

Most of the elephants are still thirsty. Some rest in the shade. The elephants will need to travel to find more water.

Elephant skin may look tough, but it is sensitive enough to feel an insect on it. Elephants take dust baths to protect their skin from the sun and insects.

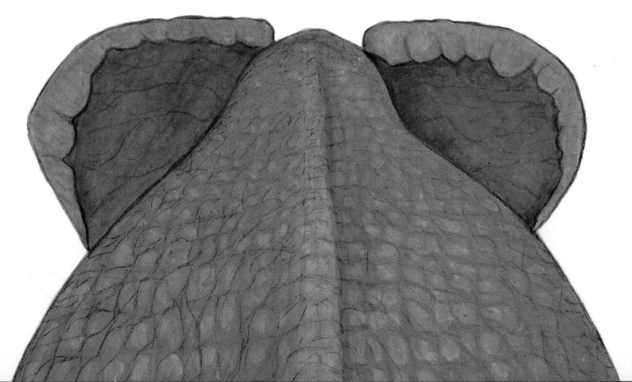

Grandmother elephant is listening again. She is listening to faraway elephants. Elephants make some sounds that people cannot hear. Other elephants can hear the sounds from miles and miles away.

Some of the elephant noises people can hear sound like rumblings from a huge stomach, or faraway thunder. Elephants cannot see as well as people, but they hear and smell very well. Smells and sounds help elephants keep in touch with each other.

Another elephant family is calling from miles away. They have found a pool of water.

The family walks toward the rumbles they heard. Near the pool, they start to run. Tons of elephant go thundering across the grassland. Elephants can run more than twenty miles an hour. That's faster than people can run.

The two families trumpet to each other as they meet. Babies chase and screech. The elephants touch trunks with their old friends. They will share the same watering hole.

The elephants drink and play for hours. They suck water into their trunks and squirt it into mouths and over dusty backs, and take baths. The elephants splash and swim. They even swim underwater, using their trunks like snorkels to breathe through.

Then they bathe in the mud. The color of an elephant family changes depending on the color of the mud or dust they bathe in. Elephants can look orange or brown when they are covered with orange or brown mud. But underneath, their skin is gray.

One baby elephant gets stuck in the mud. Two older sisters pull and push their baby brother to lift him out.

The baby brother will leave the family when he is grown. Adult male elephants wander alone, or join herds of male elephants for a while. They rejoin families only for short times.

A herd of male elephants comes to the pool to drink. Many small groups of elephants may gather together for a while in a large herd. But female elephants spend most of their time with just their own group or family. The older female elephants take care of the younger elephants. The oldest and wisest female leads the family.

Elephants can wander into places where people live, looking for food. The elephants may get into crops, gardens, even houses. Some elephants have been killed because they destroyed people's food. But many more elephants have been killed for their ivory tusks. From 1980 to 1990 over half the elephants in Africa were killed.

The people who kill elephants look for the biggest tusks. Families are left without the bigger, older elephants who lead them.

Now many people are trying to protect elephants. And people try not to buy things that are made from the ivory elephant tusks.

One elephant tusk could be sold for thousands of dollars.

There are two kinds of elephants on earth—African elephants and Asian elephants. They live in different parts of the world. Asian elephants have smaller ears than African elephants, and only males have tusks you can easily see.

Some Asian elephants live with people and haul logs and other heavy loads. But wild Asian elephants live in families, too.

African elephant   Asian elephant

Mammoths were ancient elephants
that lived in North America, Africa, Europe,
and Asia five million years ago.

Elephants have lived in their families for millions of years. With
people's help, elephant families will live on earth for many, many
years to come.